My
Earth & Space Science
Library

A World of Water

Lisa J. Amstutz

Rourke
Educational Media

A Division of
Carson
Dellosa
Education

BEFORE AND DURING READING ACTIVITIES

Before Reading: *Building Background Knowledge and Vocabulary*

Building background knowledge can help children process new information and build upon what they already know. Before reading a book, it is important to tap into what children already know about the topic. This will help them develop their vocabulary and increase their reading comprehension.

Questions and Activities to Build Background Knowledge:

1. Look at the front cover of the book and read the title. What do you think this book will be about?
2. What do you already know about this topic?
3. Take a book walk and skim the pages. Look at the table of contents, photographs, captions, and bold words. Did these text features give you any information or predictions about what you will read in this book?

Vocabulary: *Vocabulary Is Key to Reading Comprehension*

Use the following directions to prompt a conversation about each word.

- Read the vocabulary words.
- What comes to mind when you see each word?
- What do you think each word means?

Vocabulary Words:
- *ocean*
- *streams*
- *surface*
- *wells*

During Reading: *Reading for Meaning and Understanding*

To achieve deep comprehension of a book, children are encouraged to use close reading strategies. During reading, it is important to have children stop and make connections. These connections result in deeper analysis and understanding of a book.

 Close Reading a Text

During reading, have children stop and talk about the following:

- Any confusing parts
- Any unknown words
- Text to text, text to self, text to world connections
- The main idea in each chapter or heading

Encourage children to use context clues to determine the meaning of any unknown words. These strategies will help children learn to analyze the text more thoroughly as they read.

When you are finished reading this book, turn to the last page for an **After Reading Activity**.

Table of Contents

Water, Water Everywhere! 4

Bodies of Water 12

The Water Cycle 18

Photo Glossary 22

Activity 23

Index 24

After Reading Activity 24

About the Author 24

Water, Water Everywhere!

Water is all around us. It is in the air and on land. It is inside us too!

All living things need water.
They cannot live without it.

In some places, people dig **wells** to find water to drink.

9

Water covers more of Earth's **surface** than land.

Look at the picture of Earth. It is mostly blue. The blue places are water.

Most of this water is in the **ocean**.

Bodies of Water

Oceans are huge areas of water.

The water in them is salty.

Salt water is not good to drink.

Water flows in rivers and **streams**.

The water in them is fresh water.

People and animals can drink it.

Lakes hold fresh water too.

People boat, fish, and swim in lakes.

A pond is a small lake.

The Water Cycle

The sun warms up water.

Water rises into the air.

Water rises.

Water

Water cools as it rises.

It forms clouds.

Then, it falls back to Earth as rain or snow.

Cool water makes clouds.

Water falls to Earth.

Water rises.

The circle begins again.

Water

ocean (OH-shuhn): One of several bodies of salt water that covers much of the surface of the earth.

streams (streems): Flowing bodies of water, such as brooks or small rivers.

surface (SUR-fis): The outermost layer of something, as in the surface of Earth.

wells (wels): Deep holes in the ground from which you can remove water.

22

Water Cycle in a Bottle

Watch the water cycle happen in a bottle!

Supplies

clear plastic bottle with a lid

water

blue food coloring

Directions

1. Fill the bottle one-third full of water.
2. Add several drops of food coloring to the water.
3. Put the lid on your bottle. Set it in the sun.
4. Observe: What happens to the water as it warms up?
5. Now, set your bottle in a cool place.
6. Observe: What happens when the water cools?

Index

air 4, 19
clouds 20
lake(s) 16
land 4, 10
pond 16
rivers 14

About the Author

Lisa J. Amstutz is the author of more than 100 children's books. She loves learning about science and sharing fun facts with kids. Lisa lives on a small farm with her family, two goats, a flock of chickens, and a dog named Daisy.

After Reading Activity

On a map, find the body of water closest to your home. Learn as much as you can about it. How big is it? Where does the water come from? Is the water fresh or salty?

Library of Congress PCN Data

A World of Water / Lisa J. Amstutz
(My Earth and Space Science Library)
ISBN (hard cover)(alk. paper) 978-1-73163-842-7
ISBN (soft cover) 978-1-73163-919-6
ISBN (e-Book) 978-1-73163-996-7
ISBN (e-Pub) 978-1-73164-073-4
Library of Congress Control Number: 2020930192

Rourke Educational Media
Printed in the United States of America
01-1662011937

© 2021 Rourke Educational Media

www.rourkeeducationalmedia.com

Edited by: Hailey Scragg
Cover design by: Rhea Magaro-Wallace
Interior design by: Jen Bowers
Photo Credits: Cover logo: frog © Eric Phol, test tube © Sergey Lazarev, cover tab art © siridhata, cover photo ©, p4 © Peopleimages, p5 © praetorianphoto, p6 boy © Imgorthand, dog © Lorenzo Patoia, girl © Riccardo Lennart Niels Mayer, p7 cat © Grybanov, leopard © ePhotocorp, boy © Goldcastle7, girl © Lisa5201, p8 water © Pineapple Studio, dirt © t_kimura, p9 © leonello, p10 © jhorrocks, p11 © FangXiaNuo, p12 © wundervisuals, p12 & 13 © anyaberkut, p13 © Drazen, p14 © monkeybusinessimages, p15 © David Sucsy, p16 water © Pineapple Studio, boys © Sohadiszno, p17 boy & girl © Bartosz Hadyniak, p18 © golero, p19 & 20 © shutterstock, p21 © shironosov. All interior images from istockphoto.com and shutterstock.com.